Fruits and Vegetables
Coloring Book

Lynda E. Chandler

DOVER PUBLICATIONS, INC.
Mineola, New York

Introduction

This collection of 45 beautiful drawings showcases a variety of fruits and vegetables from many climates. They can be divided into three broad groups—fruits (with a sizable subgroup, the tropical fruits), fruits usually treated as vegetables, and true vegetables.

About 1,200 of the more than 3,000 identified species of tropical fruit are native to the Americas. They fascinated, amazed, and delighted some of the Spanish soldiers, priests, and settlers who arrived in the Caribbean, Central America, South America, Mexico, and what now is the southwestern United States after 1492. Some of them chronicled their first impressions of these fruits, and others drew them. From their earliest voyages, the Spaniards brought with them other tropical fruits native to Africa and Asia. Among the eleven tropical fruits featured in this book, the avocado, guava, kiwi, papaya, passion fruit, and pineapple are native to Latin America. The banana, carambola, grapefruit, mango, and orange are imports that have been popular in the Americas for centuries. All of these have become increasingly available in North American markets, especially as large numbers of Latin Americans have migrated northward.

Classifying fruits by their structure, five of those included in this book are typical berries—small, fleshy fruits that usually have many seeds within them. (Currants and grapes are berries, but neither blackberries nor raspberries are true berries; each "berry" actually is a cluster of tiny fruits, or "drupelets." Strawberries, classed as "accessory fruits," are unique in their structure; each black speck on the outside is a tiny, single-seeded fruit—an "achene.") The kiwi fruit is a large berry or capsule. The watermelon is included among the "pepos"—large, long berries with hard rinds. "Hesperidium" is the term for a citrus fruit (considered to be a berry with a leathery rind), including oranges and grapefruit. Figs and pineapples are classed as "multiple fruits." (Each "eye" of the pineapple indicates a separate fruitlet.) Apples and pears are called pome accessory fruits; cherries and peaches are "drupes," which means that they have a stony seed.

The fruits usually treated as vegetables that are described in this book—other than the tomato, which is not only a fruit, but a berry!—are asparagus, beans, corn, cucumbers, eggplant, okra, peppers (both sweet and hot varieties), pumpkins, and crookneck summer squash. Of the fruits and vegetables shown in this book, that leaves only artichokes, cabbage, carrots, lettuce, onions, potatoes, radishes, sweet potatoes, and turnips in the category of true vegetables. Carrots and the last three named are root vegetables—the edible part is a taproot that grows underground. Potatoes are tubers—the swollen end of an underground stem. More than 20 potatoes may grow on a single plant. Cabbage and lettuce are leafy vegetables, while onions are bulbs that grow underground. Artichokes are immature flower heads.

Many vegetable crops are known to have been cultivated in ancient Egypt more than 5,000 years ago, and there is evidence that some crops were cultivated in Central America about 7,000 years ago. Vegetable crops were introduced from their places of origin to other lands. This process became more rapid after 1400, when European ocean voyages became longer, during the so-called Age of Exploration. For example, the Spaniards planted cucumbers in their American colonies after 1500, and took potatoes back to Europe. Artichokes and pumpkins also were imported to Europe. Peppers were brought to Spain from the West Indies around 1525 and tomatoes from South America reached Italy by 1550. Carrots, peas, and cabbage were brought from Europe to North America by the early 1600s.

Most fresh vegetables are composed of more than 70 percent water, and contain relatively little protein (except for beans and peas) and even less fat. Potatoes and sweet potatoes supply ample carbohydrates. Vegetables supply many minerals needed by the human body. Dark-green leafy vegetables are sources of vitamin C and of carotene, a substance that the body converts into vitamin A. Carotene also is found in orange-colored vegetables—carrots being the star in that group!

ACKNOWLEDGMENT: Clara Inés Olaya graciously shared interesting perspectives on tropical fruits of the Americas, from her research for two lively, informative books on that subject that she authored (available in Spanish).

Bibliographical Note

Fruits and Vegetables Coloring Book is a new work, first published by Dover Publications, Inc., in 2001.

International Standard Book Number

ISBN-13: 978-0-486-41543-7
ISBN-10: 0-486-41543-0

Manufactured in the United States by Courier Corporation
41543005   2014
www.doverpublications.com

Apple (*Malus* species) Apples, the most popular fruit in the United States ("As American as apple pie"), starred in folkloric stories of Johnny Appleseed (actually John Chapman), who wandered Ohio and Indiana planting trees. Red, yellow, or green apple skins cover the white flesh. Some newer varieties of apples, developed in New Zealand, Japan, and the United States, are the Braeburn, the Gala, the Fuji, the Pacific Rose, and the Pink Lady. Earlier, the vibrant-green Granny Smith, grown in South Africa, quickly became popular. France and the United States are the biggest producers of apples. Besides serving as "an apple for the teacher" and a tasty snack, apples are made into juice, cider, wine, brandy, applesauce, apple butter, jelly, and vinegar. They are rich in vitamins A and C.

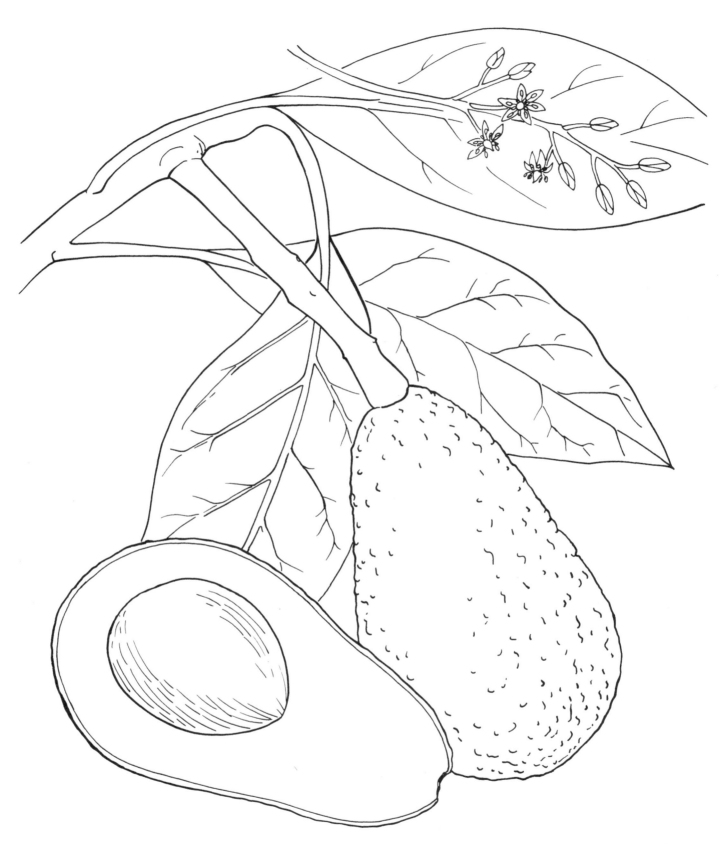

Avocado *(Persea americana)* Avocados flourished in the rich soil on the slopes of Central American volcanos. By 1500, the trees grew from Mexico to Peru. In Nicaragua, they were popular wedding gifts. A Spaniard wrote in 1519, ". . . what it has inside is [smooth] like butter and is wonderfully flavorful . . ."

Avocado oil is used in making fine soaps, and it is a good hair conditioner. If a pin is stuck into the large seed, a reddish-brown fluid comes out. The Spanish conquerors used this indelible tint to write letters, and people still use it as a laundry marker. In Brazil and France the avocado is eaten with sugar, as a dessert.

Banana *(Musa sapientum)* Bananas were cultivated in Malaysia more than 4,000 years ago. Later, they were planted in Africa and were taken to India and the Middle East by Arab traders. The Portuguese brought them to the Canary Islands, in the Atlantic Ocean west of Africa. From there, Columbus took some on his second voyage to the Caribbean. One plant (which is an herb, not a tree) will produce about 150 fruits on a single stem. After the stem is cut the plant dies, but another stem grows from the same horizontal root.

Blackberry (*Rubus fruticosus*) The blackberry grows on a prickly bush found most commonly in the eastern United States and in Pacific Coast areas. Its leaves are oval-shaped, with serrated edges. The flowers may be white, pink, or red. The black or reddish-purple fruits consist of clusters of tiny drupelets (tiny stony-seeded fruits). Blackberries provide moderate amounts of vitamin C and iron.

Blueberry *(Vaccinium corymbosum)* These small, juicy berries are dark blue, with a slightly waxy-looking surface. They are popular in jams, tarts, and muffins. Blueberries are a good source of vitamin C and iron. They grow only in acidic, moist soils. New Jersey is the leading state where blueberries are cultivated, but they also are grown in parts of Michigan and North Carolina. Wild blueberries are picked in many other areas.

Carambola *(Averrhoa carambola)* This shrub, native to Malaysia, grows to a height of 15 feet and produces small, five-petaled magenta blossoms. The leaves are maroon when young, but turn green as they grow larger. The yellow or golden-brown fruit may be as much as 5 inches long. Each fruit has 3 to 5 deep ribs. Because of the form of a slice of this fruit, which resembles that of a starfish, it also is called star fruit. There are both sweet and sour varieties.

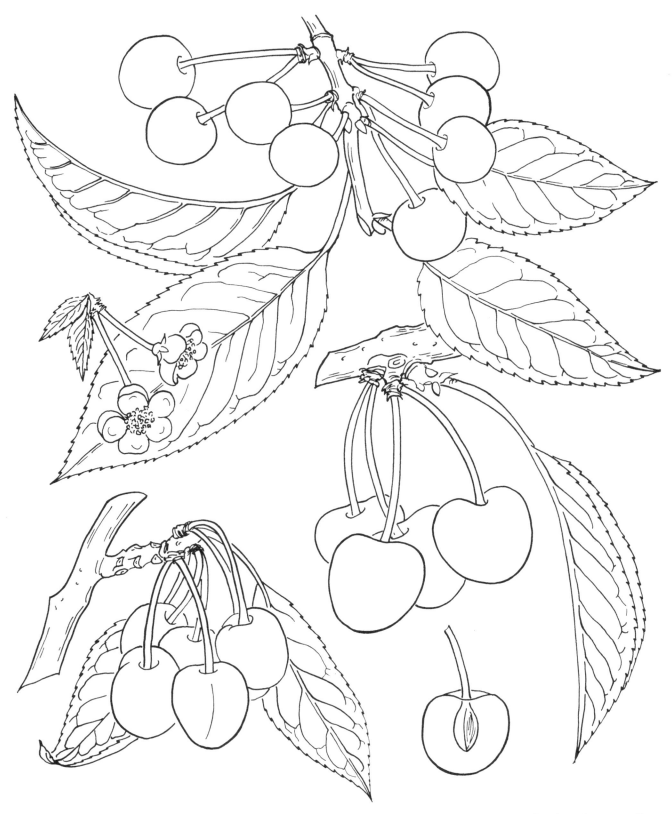

Cherry (*Prunus avium*) North America and Europe each are home to about a dozen species of cherries, but eastern Asia is home to many more. Cherry-blossom time is very important in Japan. However, cherries originated in western Asia and eastern Europe, then spread throughout Europe. Sweet cherries grow on trees that grow to more than twice the height of those that bear sour cherries, which are so acidic that they usually are not eaten fresh. Large quantities of sour cherries are canned or frozen, after being suitably sweetened. The U.S. cherry crop is the world's largest, but this good source of vitamin A is grown on every continent except Africa.

Cranberry (*Vaccinium macrocarpum*) The northern cranberry is mainly consumed in the United States and Canada, in the form of canned (often jellied) sweet-and-tart sauce and bottled juice. The large berries vary from pink to dark red; there are some red-and-white varieties. Cranberry bogs have peaty soil with sand on top. They are flooded in winter to prevent freezing of the vines. Rhode Island, Massachusetts, New Jersey, and Wisconsin are the states where this acidic berry is grown in quantity; it also is harvested near the coasts of Washington and Oregon. The dark-red southern cranberry, or red huckleberry, is grown in the Appalachian mountains of the southeast.

Black Currant *(Ribes nigrum)*; American **Red Currant** *(Ribes vulgare)* Currants are berries that grow on perennial shrubs found on every continent, but most commonly all over North America and in most of Eurasia. They thrive in cool, moist climates, and even grow near the Arctic Circle! Popular jellies and preserves are made from currants, which are rich in vitamin C, calcium, phosphorus, and iron.

Fig *(Ficus carica)* The fig was one of the earliest fruit trees cultivated by humans. It was grown across a wide band of Asia, from Turkey to north India, and also in Mediterranean countries. Figs sustained the vigorous Spartans and citizens of other ancient Greek city-states. Smyrna figs, introduced in California, were not cultivated successfully until 1899, when tiny fig wasps were imported to pollinate them. To pollinate, the wasp enters a very small hole in the fruit (the enlarged end of the flower stem), which contains hundreds of miniature florets. Each floret develops into a fruitlet with one seed, inside the fig's papery sac.

Gooseberry *(Ribes hirtellum)* Gooseberries are grown and eaten fresh, as well as in recipes, in Great Britain and some northern European countries much more than in the United States and Canada. However, they have been used in preserves, pies, and tarts since colonial days in North America. This and several other edible American species grow red berries on a hardy plant in cool or cold, moist climates. A cultivated patch produces fruit for ten to twenty years.

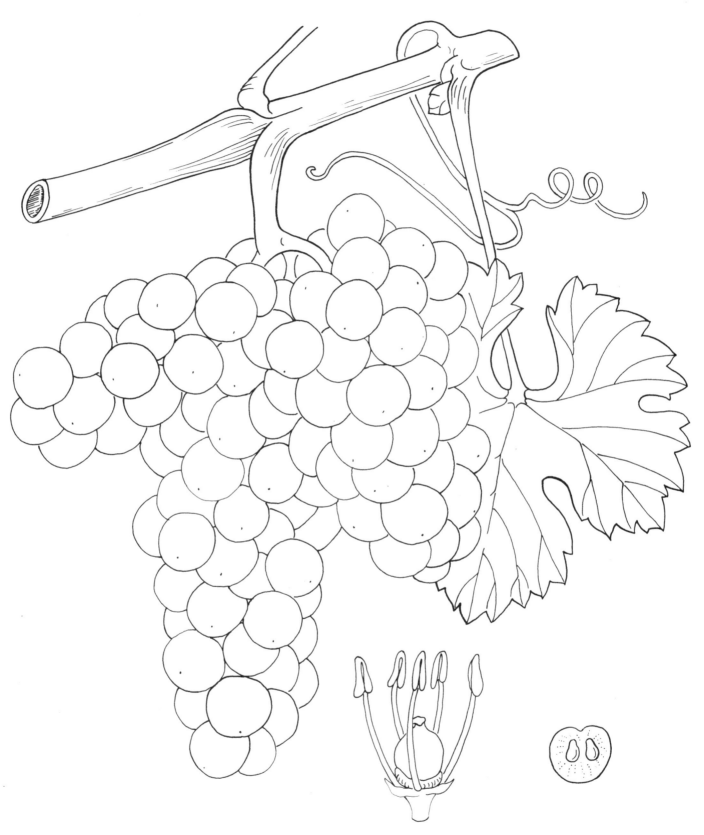

Red Grape (*Vitis palmata*) The biblical Book of Genesis reports that Noah planted a vineyard and became drunk after consuming some of the wine produced. There are about 60 species and 8,000 varieties of grape, but raisins (dried grapes) mainly are made from only three varieties, and in the United States bottled juice is made from only one variety. California is the U.S. state where winemaking is a major industry, but New York State also has a winery region. All grapes contain glucose and fructose; those with more glucose are easier to ferment.

Guava *(Psidium guajava)* In fertile land, a guava tree will grow from each seed cast on the ground, as a Spanish chronicler noted in amazement in Santo Domingo in 1568. On the Caribbean islands, the Taínos made wine from the fruit, and from the leaves they made a syrup to relieve stomachache. The wood was used to make bows and arrows. Guavas have more vitamin C than oranges do. Pastes, jellies, and nectars are made from the fruit.

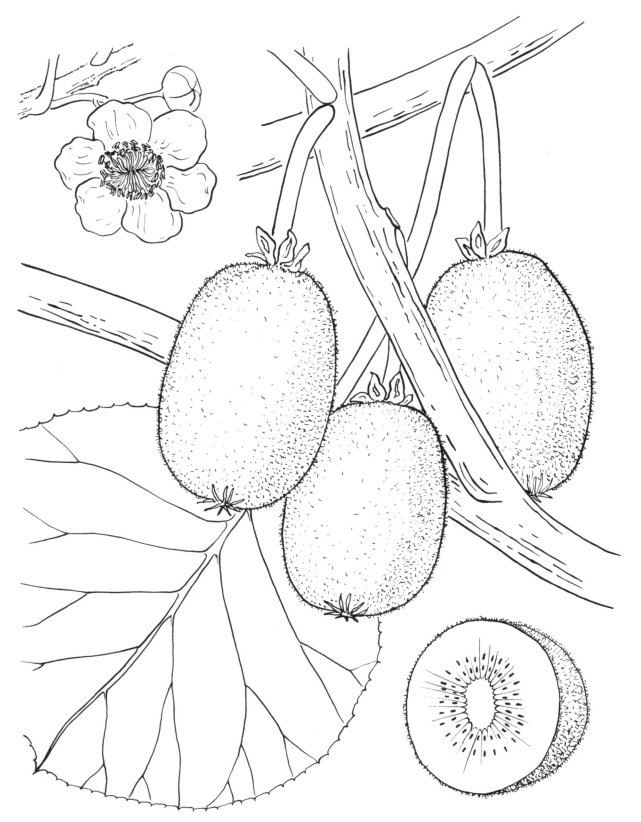

Kiwi *(Actinidia chinensis)* The kiwi, a vine that produces oval berries or capsules, originated in southeast China. Also called the Chinese gooseberry, it grows in tropical America as well as in tropical and temperate Asia. The fruit, about 2 inches long, contains 15 times more vitamin C than an orange. It got its name because its furry brown exterior was said to resemble the scruffy plumage of the brown kiwi bird, native to New Zealand, the biggest producer of the fruit. The flowers are yellow, with a green ring around a yellow center. The large leaves are heart-shaped. The fruit's crisp, emerald-green pulp contains many small black seeds around a white, firmer center. Kiwi ice cream, pies, and wine are made.

Mango *(Mangifera indica)* The sweet, piquant mango has been a delightful refreshment in India for more than 4,000 years. The juicy fruit was sacred to Hindus as well as to Buddhists. The Mughal emperor Akbar (reigned 1556–1605), who conquered much of India, ordered that 100,000 mango trees be planted by his palace. An oriole native to India is called the mango bird, and an entire genus of hummingbirds is named "mango." There are 30 varieties of mangoes, some of which are hybrids. Some are about the size of a lemon, others are too big to be encircled by a large hand. Mango is used in chutney (a sweet-and-tart condiment), ice cream, and sherbet.

Sweet Orange (*Citrus sinensis*) and **Grapefruit** (*Citrus paradisi*) The orange tree, from its earliest home in China more than 4,000 years ago, was brought by Arab traders to Africa and then to Spain. Spanish conquerors planted orange trees in Latin America in the 16th century. The grapefruit may have originated in Jamaica. Trees grow to majestic sizes, producing large quantities of fruit amid glossy, dark-green leaves. The fruit, 4 to 6 inches in diameter, has a juicy pulp, pale yellow in color, or pink in some varieties. About 80 percent of the world's grapefruit are grown in four U.S. states. The United States also has the most orange groves in the world.

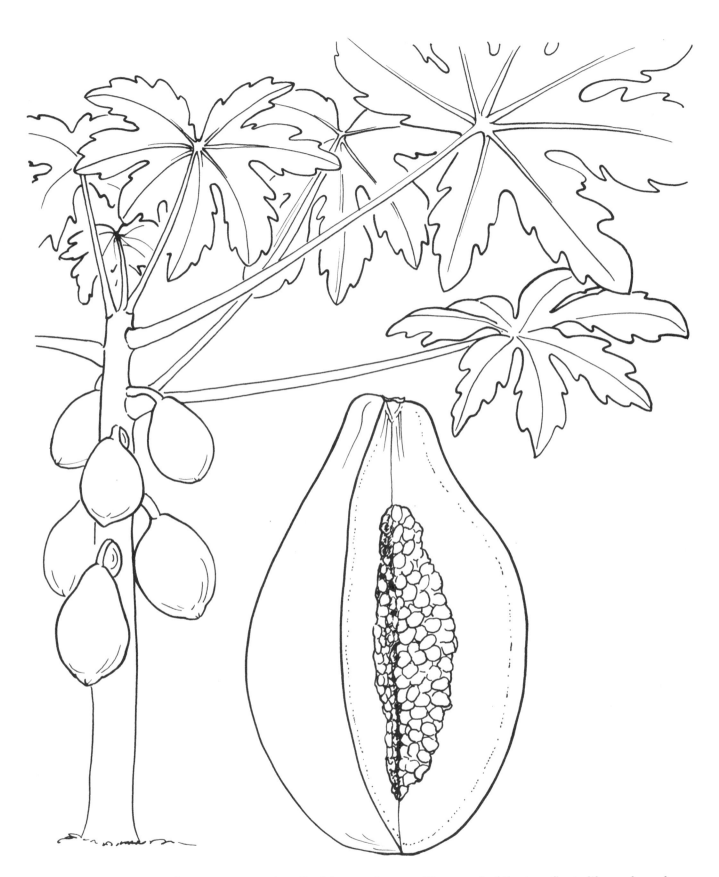

Papaya *(Carica papaya)* The papaya tree is tall, thin, and straight, with no branches except at the top. The fruits grow to be as big as melons. Fernández de Oviedo, a foremost chronicler of the Caribbean lands invaded by Spain, noticed in 1547 that they ripen one by one. The wood of the tree floats like cork, and was used to make rafts. The papaya fruit contains a substance called papain, which aids human digestion, tenderizes meat cooked with slices of the fruit, and is used in pharmaceutical products, to clarify beer, etc.

Passion Fruit (*Passiflora edulis*) The passion fruit got its name because some Spaniards in 16th-century Latin America expressed the idea that the parts of its flower can be thought of as symbols of the Passion of Christ.

The pulp of the passion fruit is very fragrant. It is a watery yellow in color, and contains many acidic gray seeds. Mixed with sugared water, the pulp makes a refreshing drink.

Peach (*Prunus persica*) Like apple and pear trees, peach trees are in the rose family. The juicy fruit, which may have yellow, white, or red flesh, contrasts with long, glossy green leaves. An indentation curves from the stem to the base of the fuzzy-skinned fruit, showing the boundary between the two original parts from which the peach grows. Peach trees thrive in warm temperate climates. They probably originated in China and slowly spread westward. Spaniards brought peach trees to Nueva España (now Mexico) by 1600. Worldwide, peaches rank behind apples and pears as a major fruit crop. In U.S. orchards, only apples outrank them. Peaches are cultivated on every continent, from South Africa to Italy to Argentina to Australia.

Pear *(Pyrus communis)* The flesh of the pear generally is softer and sweeter than that of the apple. Also, the white fruit includes "stone cells" or "grit" in its composition, which gives it a slightly grainy texture. The pear's skin ranges in color from pale yellow through various shades of green to a bronze green. The shape of the fruit varies according to the variety. Bartlett, Bosc, and Anjou are some of the most popular varieties available in the United States. Jelly is made from the quince pear. In Europe, much of the pear crop is fermented to produce perry, an alcoholic beverage. Pear trees, which are relatively tall and long-lived, grow in temperate climates on every continent. The flowers, usually white, are similar to apple blossoms.

Pineapple (*Ananas comosus*) In 1547, Fernández de Oviedo marveled that the pineapple's ". . . fragrance is so penetrating that when a fruit is in a house, the whole street smells of it . . ." Its origin was in Brazil, where native peoples used it to make wine and a medicine for bronchitis. After the plant was taken to Spain, it became coveted by European royalty and, as a symbol of hospitality, was carved near doors of inns and private homes. The fruit usually rotted before reaching Europe from America, though. Charles II of England confronted this by having pineapples grown in hothouses. Then, after two years had elapsed, he gave a splendid banquet featuring the fruit. (Each plant produces only one pineapple, every two years.) The major growers are in the Hawaiian islands and in Puerto Rico and some other Caribbean islands.

Raspberry *(Rubus idaeus)* Stakes or trellises are used to support the "cane" of this bush as it grows. The plants bear white flowers with about twenty yellow stamens, and have short, slender prickles on their stems. Both red and black raspberries *(Rubus leuco)* are grown extensively in the United States, in several Mid-Atlantic, North Central, and Northwestern states. Purple raspberries and other, rarer color varieties are not cultivated much. Raspberries were being cultivated in Great Britain by the early 1600s, but wild raspberries evolved much earlier, probably in eastern Asia, and were being enjoyed in Italy around the time of Christ.

Strawberry *(Fragaria ananasa)* The three-part leaves of this low-growing herbaceous plant have sharply serrated edges and are hairy. The five-petaled flowers are white. The "fruit" (really an enlarged flower receptacle) is red on the outside, and red or white on the inside, according to its degree of ripeness. The tiny black specks on the outside (achenes) are the actual fruit. Both fresh and frozen strawberries are marketed. Strawberry jam is very popular, and strawberries brighten many desserts, such as the U.S. favorite, strawberry shortcake. In the Americas strawberries are grown from Canada to Patagonia. They also are cultivated in Europe, Australia, New Zealand, and Japan. In the wild, birds and bears enjoy them.

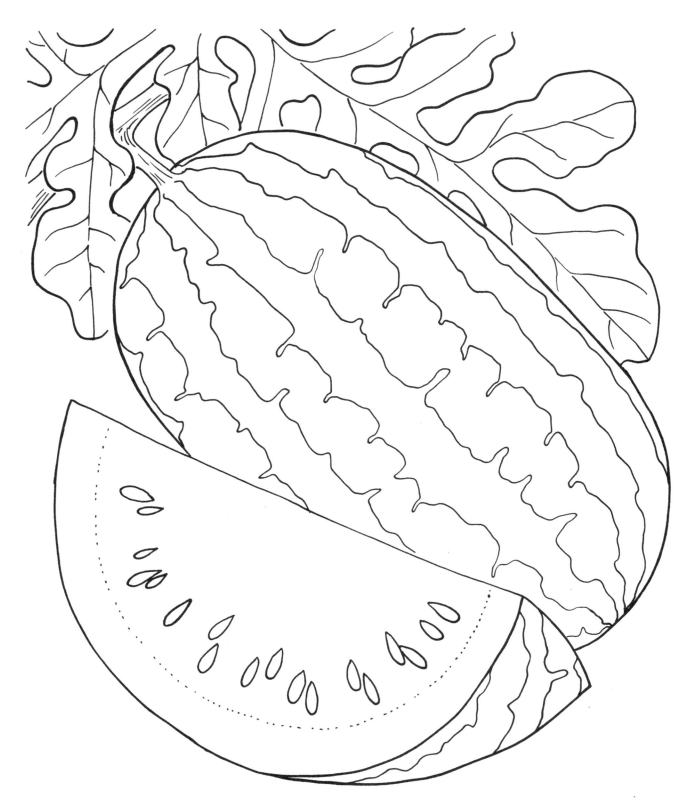

Watermelon *(Citrullus lanatus)* Art and literature indicate that watermelon were grown in India and in Egypt more than 4,000 years ago. This succulent fruit of the gourd family is native to tropical Africa. It grows along the ground on a vine, which produces 2 to 15 fruits at a time. The oblong, thick-rinded fruit may weigh as little as 2 pounds or as much as 45. The colors of the skin, rind, and flesh vary, but generally the skin is green, the rind is white, and the flesh is pink to red in color, with many large, nearly flat, oblong black seeds embedded in it. Watermelon is popular as a refreshing treat on a hot day, and is associated with Fourth of July picnics and barbecues in the United States. Pickled watermelon rind is tasty, too. In its wild form, this species is an important source of food and water in desert areas of southern Africa.

Artichoke *(Cynara scolymus)* Artichokes first were grown in the lands around the Mediterranean Sea. For centuries the young leaves were eaten. The modern form, of which the immature flower heads are edible, was being consumed in Italy by 1400. If the flower bud is not picked to be eaten, and instead fully develops, thousands of tiny purple flowers, like those on thistle plants, develop in a large "head." Artichokes (and sometimes just the tender "heart") are served both hot and cold, in a variety of dishes, and are popular marinated.

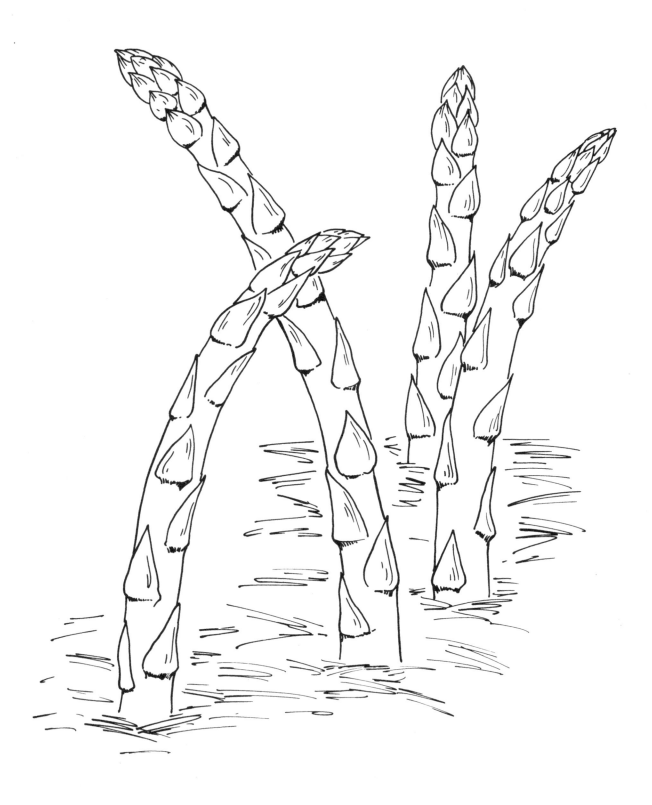

Asparagus *(Asparagus officinalis)* Garden asparagus, a member of the lily family, is one of about 300 species of asparagus, native to areas ranging from Siberia to southern Africa, including the Mediterranean lands. France, Italy, and the United States are the largest producers of asparagus, which the ancient Romans considered to be a delicacy. Asparagus may be white or green. The plant tends to be somewhat woody, but in its third year of growth it produces tender stalks and tips, preceded by small, greenish-yellow flowers. This cycle is repeated each spring for 15 to 20 years. In autumn, red berries develop. Some species (including asparagus fern, which is not a true fern) have delicate, lacy foliage used in corsages and floral sprays.

Bean *(Phaseolus vulgaris)* Many varieties of bean plants are native to Central and South America. All beans are legumes and grow inside pods. The pods of some types are edible, such as those of the kind shown here (variously called green, snap, French, or string bean) and snow-pea pods (from China). Plants with edible pods usually don't produce edible beans of good quality. Beans grow especially well when intermingled with plantings of beets or carrots. Beans (not the pods, but the seeds inside them) are marketed dry (these must be soaked, then cooked) or precooked and canned. They are high in protein and fiber.

Beet *(Beta vulgaris)* Beets (as well as turnips and radishes) sculpted in precious metals were offered to Apollo by the ancient Greeks. The beet is a taproot. Usually it is dark red or reddish purple, both inside and out, but it may be nearly white. The sugar beet, developed in Germany in the 1700s, was promoted by Napoleon Bonaparte after 1800 to substitute for sugarcane, which at that time was grown primarily in colonies of Great Britain, France's imperial rival. Beets are high in carbohydrates and in fiber. In addition to boiled beets and beet soup (borscht), pickled beets are enjoyed by many.

Cabbage (*Brassica oleracea*, variant *capitata*) The softer form among the cabbages with a hard "head," known as Savoy cabbage, originated in the Mediterranean lands. The harder form, usually simply called "cabbage," was developed in Northern Europe during the Middle Ages. Its ancestors grew along the coasts of northern Europe more than 8,000 years ago. Heads of cabbage are sliced or shredded and eaten raw in salads (including cole slaw), cooked, and made into sauer-kraut. Cabbage leaves generally are green (often with a gray or blue tint), but a form with magenta leaves commonly is known as red cabbage. Broccoli, Brussels sprouts, cauliflower, collards, kale, and kohlrabi all are forms of cabbage *(Brassica oleracea)* of which parts other than the leaves are eaten, or in which the edible leaves do not form around a head. Ornamental cabbage (green, white, and purple bands of frilly leaves on one head) is not eaten.

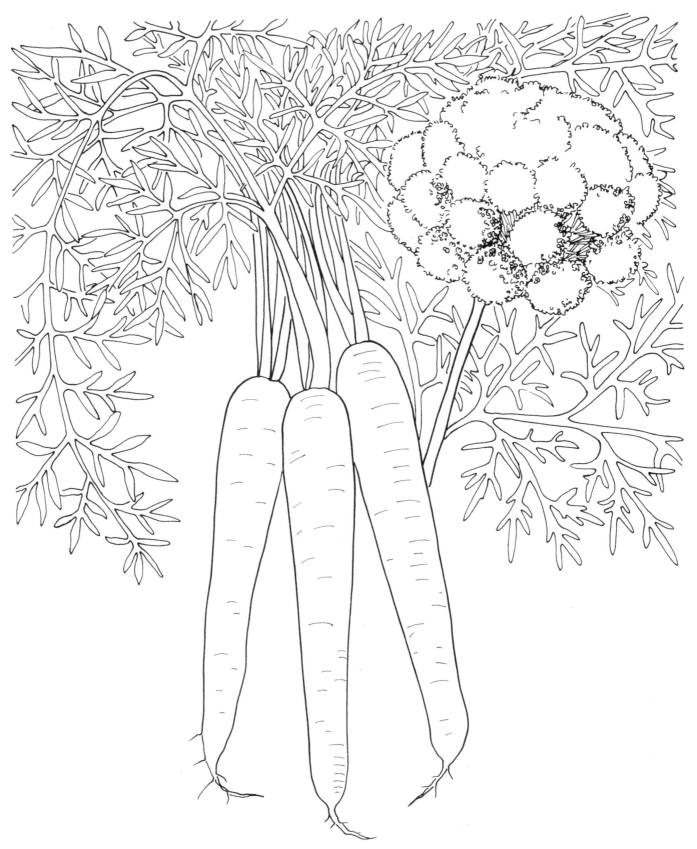

Carrot (*Daucus carota sativus*) Native to Afghanistan, the carrot is a taproot. The white flowers known as Queen Anne's Lace grow amid the green foliage on the tall stems that rise above each underground wild carrot. Although the color orange is identified with carrots, some are white, yellow, or purple. The smaller varieties are the most tender. Carrots are eaten raw as well as boiled, and made into juice and soups. They are a prime source of carotene, which is converted by humans into vitamin A.

Corn *(Zea mays)* Also known as maize, this grass is native to North, Central, and South America. Along with several varieties of beans and squash, it formed the basis of Native Americans' diet for thousands of years, in areas ranging from what now is the U.S. Southwest to South America. Currently it is second only to wheat, worldwide, as a food crop, in terms of acreage planted. Sweet corn (the only type in which the corn sugar within each kernel does not become cornstarch) is eaten roasted or boiled, on or off the cob, and is used in soups and stews. Popcorn, often served with butter and salt, is a popular snack. Like other grains, corn can be fermented to produce corn liquor.

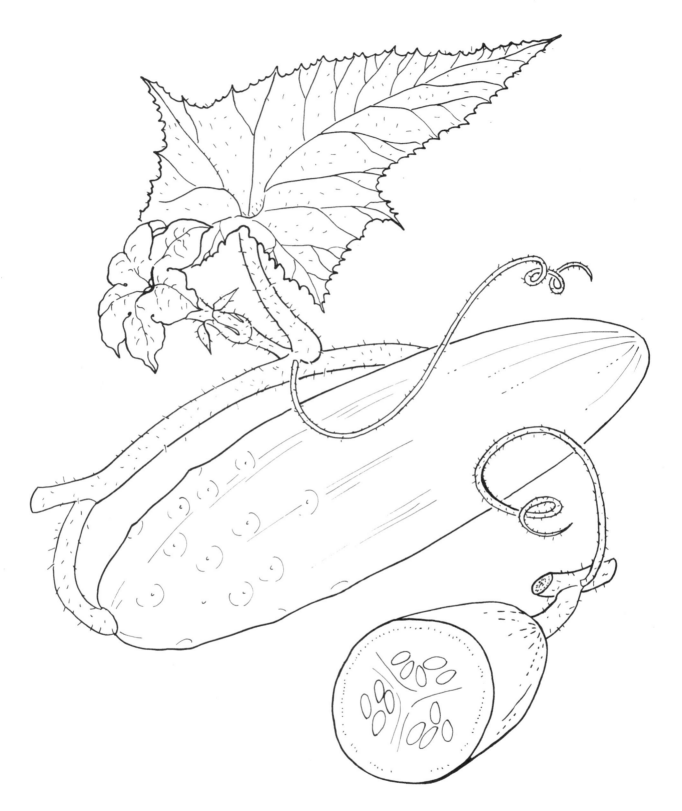

Cucumber (*Cucumis sativus*) This member of the gourd family developed in central and western China and in northern India. There are three groups of varieties of cultivated cucumbers. The first two groups, which are grown in fields and gardens and mainly used for pickling, have white and black spines, respectively, protruding from their green skin. Varieties in the third group, which are without spines, produce large fruits which are sliced or diced to be used in salads and relishes. These are grown only in greenhouses or on frames, to which the plant clings for support by means of tendrils on its rough stems. Cucumbers have little nutritional value. Each fruit contains many pale seeds, and each slice, whether a cross-section or a lengthwise strip, has several, distributed around a Y-shape central "column" within the long fruit.

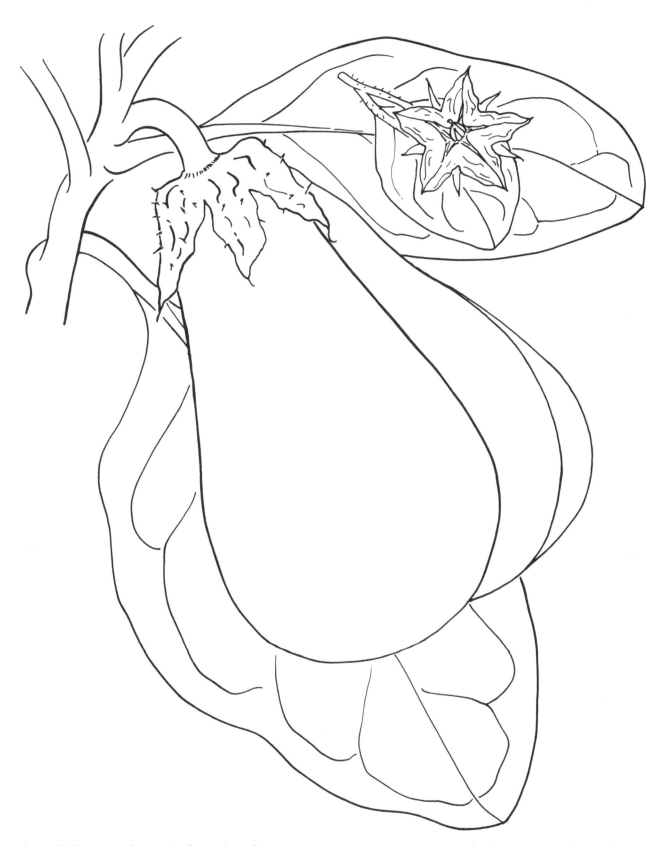

Eggplant (*Solanum melongena*) Central and western China and northern India are the ancestral homes of the cultivated eggplant. A member of the nightshade family, the eggplant is related to the potato. This plant requires a warm climate. It forms an erect stem with large leaves. This egg-shape fruit (a large berry containing many seeds) has a glossy skin, often dark purple, but sometimes red, yellow, white, or striped. The plant's flowers, about two inches wide, are violet-color. The eggplant's coarse-textured flesh is not eaten raw. The fruit is baked, fried, or roasted.

Lettuce (*Latuca sativa*) The wild ancestor of garden lettuce originated in central and western China. Many varieties have developed around the world. All of them are low in calories and high in fiber content. Some of the more common types of lettuce used in salads in North America are iceberg, Boston, romaine, and arugula. Lettuce benefits from being grown close to carrots and strawberries.

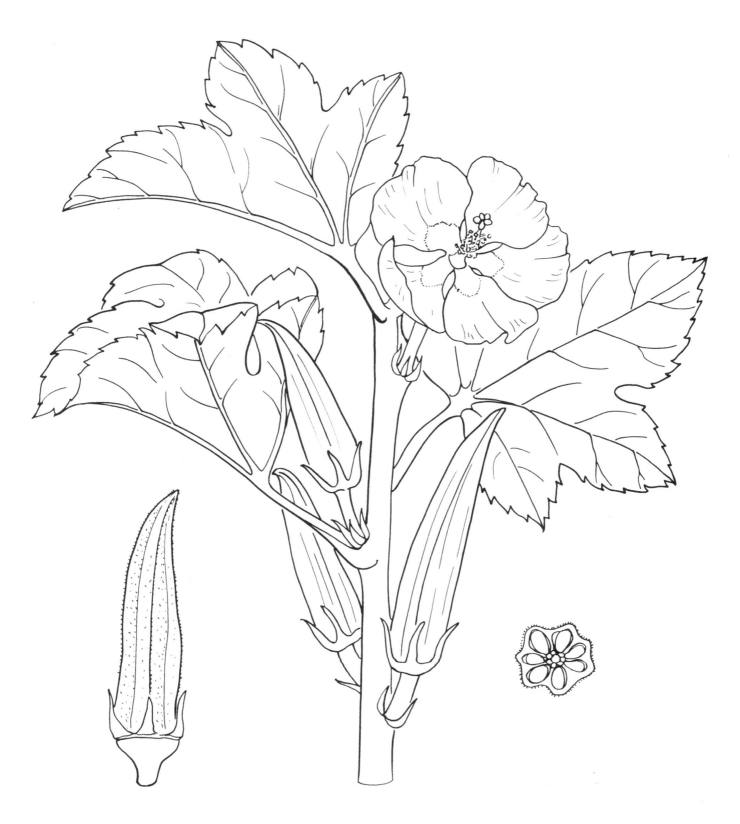

Okra *(Abelmoschus esculentus)* It is thought that the okra plant first developed in Ethiopia and then spread throughout the tropical areas of Africa and Asia. Its leaves may be 12 inches wide. The yellow flowers have a crimson center. Only the tender, immature fruit is eaten. The green fruit is in the form of a pod, 3 to 8 inches long, hairy at the base and containing many oval-shape, dark seeds. As the fruit contains much gelatinous substance, it is used as a thickener in soups and stews, including the "gumbos" served in Louisiana and other U.S. southeastern states. The okra pods, which have narrow, angular indentations down their length, also are eaten boiled or fried. This fruit was eaten by African and African-ancestry slaves in the Caribbean, where a spinach-and-okra-based stew called *callaloo* still is popular.

Onion (*Allium cepa*) Onions were cultivated in both the Mediterranean lands and in Ethiopia in prehistoric times. A record carved in the stone of the Great Pyramid at Giza states the cost for onions and garlic eaten by the slaves who built it in ancient Egypt. The edible part of the onion is a bulb—actually, fleshy leaves closely wrapped together. Scallions (left) are the tall, hollow, thin-walled cylindrical leaves that grow up from a young bulb. "Yellow," red-skinned, and Spanish onions belong to the *Allium* genus. Shallots are in the *cepa* species. Onions are used in salads, soups, sauces, and stews, and are sauteed, fried, roasted, and broiled.

Pea *(Pisum sativum)* Pea plants are native to the Mediterranean lands. The cultivated pea most popular in North America, Europe, and parts of Asia is a variety of *Pisum sativum.* The garden pea, like all beans, is a legume—an edible seed contained in a pod. The pea pod is more cylindrical than flat. The stem of this trailing plant is hollow. Tendrils that grow from the leaves enable the plant to cling to a trellis or frame. The flowers are white or purple. Garden peas are tender and have a high sugar content. Five to ten peas are enclosed in a pod, which splits in half when ripe.

Pepper (*Capsicum frutescens*) About 20 varieties of this shrubby perennial herb are native to South America. Among the *annuum* variety, five groups are the main ones cultivated in North America and northern South America. One group includes the green pepper, bell pepper, sweet pepper, and pimento, which turns from green to red or yellow when fully ripe. These are thick-walled and have many pale seeds in their hollow cavity. They have a mild flavor and are popular in salads, stuffed, sauteed, and roasted. They also are marinated and used in relishes. Another group includes the red cone pepper, which has slender fruits, about three inches long, that grow in clusters and are very pungent. A third group includes the very pungent cayenne, chili, long, and red peppers, which may be a foot long and are the source of chili powder and paprika.

Potato (*Solanum tuberosum*) Potatoes were being cultivated in the Andes mountain chain, near the west coast of South America, for at least 2,000 years before Columbus stumbled upon America. The Spaniards introduced these white-fleshed tubers (swollen underground stems) to Europe after 1550, and gradually they became a staple crop in Ireland, Germany, and western England. They are served boiled and mashed or sliced (with sauce or gravy), baked whole or baked and stuffed, fried, in potato salads of various kinds, and in stews and soups.

Pumpkin (*Cucurbita pepo*) The pumpkin, a variety of squash, is native to the Andes and Central America. Few people except pumpkin growers know that the flowers on the pumpkin vine open only once in each 24-hour period, between 5:00 and 6:00 a.m. The pulpy, sometimes stringy fruit inside the pumpkin's thick rind is enjoyed in soups and pies, and pumpkin segments are baked by themselves. Roasted pumpkin seeds are a healthful snack. The "shell" of the pumpkin can be carved into fine jack-o'-lanterns.

Radish *(Raphanus raphanistrum)* These crisp, sharp-flavored roots first grew in China and Central Asia. In Japan, 2-feet-long radishes are grown. They are eaten both fresh and pickled. Radishes, with the strong contrast in color between their dark exterior and white interior, are a favorite vegetable for craftspeople to carve. The city of Oaxaca in Mexico holds a major exhibition and contest in the plaza each year at Christmastime, displaying hundreds of Nativity scenes with figures formed entirely from radishes.

Summer crookneck squash (*Cucurbita pepo, melopepo* variety) This variety of squash is native to central and western China. Its skin is golden-yellow and "warty." The flesh is pale yellow. The biggest summer crooknecks are about 9 inches long and 3 inches wide. This squash has a tapering cylindrical shape, with a curved neck. Close relatives are the zucchini squash and the summer straightneck squash. All three varieties are used in salads, roasted, and baked in dishes such as ratatouille and vegetable lasagna.

Sweet potato *(Ipomoea batatas)* This root plant was enjoyed by the native peoples of the Caribbean islands and Central America for thousands of years before Spaniards invaded their lands. Called *batata*, it was a major source of carbohydrates, along with *yautia* and *yuca*. It is sold in some North American markets where immigrants from the Caribbean reside. The sweet potato is not actually a potato (which is a swollen stem, not a root). The plant's pink or purple blossoms resemble small morning glories. Every sweet potato has several buds embedded in the surface. Each bud, if planted, will sprout and grow into a new plant.

Tomato *(Lycopersicon esculentum)* A native of South America, taken to Europe from Mexico by Spaniards in the early 1500s, the tomato is in the nightshade family. Some leaves may be 18 inches long, but the yellow flowers, which grow in clusters, are small. The fruit is a berry, with many small seeds in pools of a jellylike or watery liquid, between fleshy walls within the fruit.

Tomatoes usually are red or yellow. They vary in size and shape, but tend toward roundness. Cherry tomatoes and egg tomatoes are named for their forms. When first grown in England, the tomato became a courtship gift, named "love apple." Pasta with tomato sauce, basic to Italian cookery, began with spaghetti from China and tomatoes from tropical America!

44

Turnip *(Brassica rapa,* Rapifera group) Probably native to central and eastern Asia, the turnip has been cultivated for thousands of years, with the coarser varieties being used for animal fodder. The turnip is closely related to the rutabaga, or Swedish turnip. Although it is suited for cool and cold climates, it does not withstand frost as well as the rutabaga. Turnip greens are eaten in salads. The turnip itself, a taproot, has pale yellow or white flesh. It is eaten boiled and mashed, baked, and in soups.

Index of Common Names

Index of Scientific Names